How To Overcome Worries Permanently And Forever In The Seven Most Vital Areas Of Your Life Starting From Today!

Succeeding In Family, Health, Financial, Educational, Professional, Social And Spiritual Areas Of Your Life

Written by
Olakunle **Solomon** Fatoye

This book is dedicated to the readers of this book.

TABLE OF CONTENTS

chapter one............5   chapter ten...........23

chapter two...........7   chapter eleven.....25

chapter three.........9   chapter twelve.....27

chapter four.........11   chapter thirteen...29

chapter five.........13   chapter fourteen. .31

chapter six...........15   chapter fifteen.....33

chapter seven......17   chapter sixteen....37

chapter eight.......19   about the author. .43

chapter nine.........21

CHAPTER ONE

HOW TO OVERCOME WORRIES PERMANENTLY AND
FOREVER IN THE SEVEN MOST VITAL AREAS OF
YOUR LIFE STARTING FROM TODAY!

HOW TO OVERCOME WORRIES!

GET WISDOM! GET RID OF WORRIES!

WHAT IS WORRY?

Simply stated, worry can be defined as "a state of mental and
emotional agitation and distress resulting from undue concern
over something impending or anticipated".

Worry involves an uneasiness of mind or a brooding anxiety
about a real or imagined situation or possibility.

It is an unresolved feeling of fretful apprehension and mental
unrest which is a close companion of fear, anxiety, stress,
insecurity, and tension.

Worry is translated "anxiety or care". It is taken from a Greek word which literally means, "to divide, rip or tear apart".

It aptly describes the torturous effects of worry which tear our heart, mind, and emotions.

CHAPTER TWO

WHO SUFFERS FROM WORRY?

Everyone!

Worry is so prevalent and widespread in todays society that it has reached epidemic proportions.

Worry is one of the greatest problems affecting mankind.

Everyone experiences worry in some degree of intensity and duration during their life.

No one is exempted or totally immune.

Worry afflicts both young and old, children and adults, men and women, rich and poor, educated and uneducated, healthy and unhealthy, godly and ungodly.

It is a universal problem which cuts across every conceivable social, ethnic, and racial barrier.

Worry is such a commonplace problem that it has been referred to as the "official emotion of our age", and "the most pervasive psychological phenomenon of our time".

It stands out as one of the greatest sources of human suffering and distress.

CHAPTER THREE

WHAT ARE THE EFFECTS OF WORRY?

Worry can produce a wide variety of destructive symptoms, which can aggravate our mental, emotional, physical, and spiritual well being.

The following are evident; mental and emotional fatigue, ulcers, migraines, drug and alcohol dependence, frequent headaches, hypertension, loss of appetite, backaches, nervousness, lack of concentration, insomnia, stomach problems, skin rashes, etc.

Worry can paralyze us with fear, confusion, and insecurity.

It can cripple our faith, courage and belief and undermine our joy, peace of mind and our sense of contentment.

Worry can destroy our physical, mental and spiritual enthusiasm, motivation and energy.

It can cause us to withdraw from life, become antisocial, and sink into depression.

It can stifle our creativity, dull our personality, and distort our judgment.

As we can see, worry breeds a whole host of harmful consequences, which can hinder our well-being if not handled properly.

CHAPTER FOUR

COMMON CAUSES OF WORRY.

UNCERTAINTY ABOUT THE FUTURE.

An anxious anticipation about future uncertainties is a major cause of worry.

We live in a world of constant change, unrest, and instability.

The current climate of international tension generates a constant undercurrent of apprehension.

This tends to reinforce an atmosphere of worry, insecurity, and uncertainty concerning the possibilities of tomorrow.

The arms race, the threat of nuclear holocaust, the growing crime rate, the ever-changing economic scene, political upheaval, and the "doomsday" forecasts both within and without create a mental environment conducive for breeding worry and apprehension.

Whether our worry involves the minor consequences of life or major life-changing possibilities, our ability to pay a bill or our chances of surviving a nuclear holocaust, the uncertainty about the conditions of tomorrow stands out as the greatest, single source of worry.

CHAPTER FIVE

THE CARES OF THIS WORLD.

Being overly concerned with the cares of this life is also a major cause of worry.

The concerns of this present life often intensify the potential for unrest, anxiety, and wholesome worry.

This is especially true in our materialistic age.

We live in a world of great value systems, demands, and expectations.

We are constantly harassed and bombarded by enticements and influences which promote cares and encourage us to measure up to the standards of success and security which the world embraces.

Some succumb to unnecessary worry because they are overly anxious and agitated about the concern of this present life.

Instead of realising the basic fact that wisdom reveals the

shortness of any mans life no matter how well prolonged it is, many are overwhelmed with worry about making a living, acquiring possessions, saving for the future, achieving material expectations, or keeping up with the Joneses.

CHAPTER SIX

THE PRESSURES OF LIFE.

The pressures of life are a close companion to the cares of this world.

The challenges, concerns, and complexities of modern life exert tremendous pressures upon us which can overwhelm us with worry and anxiety.

The unrelenting demands of our pressure cooker world, the constant crush of responsibilities, and the never ending strain of meeting dead-lines, achieving goals, or fulfilling expectation can often create a state of stress and worry concerning our ability to meet the obligation of life.

CHAPTER SEVEN

THE PAST INFLUENCES AND EXPERIENCES.

A persons present worries are often the result of past conditioning.

Many are victimised by repeated episodes of worry due to the contributing factors from their past.

Yesterdays worries often lay the groundwork for todays anxieties, previous fears, insecurities, disappointments, traumas, and problems can create a sensitivity in certain areas of our life which manifests itself in the future through re-occurring bouts of worry.

Children can subtly acquire a specific pattern of re-occurring worry due to repeated exposure to their parents influence.

For example, if their parents suffered from financial distress and upheaval, a child may grow up with a tendency to nurse financial insecurity and worry.

If the parents were overly anxious about health problems, a child may grow up with exaggerated anxieties and hypochondria in this area also.

Whatever the cause or source of past worries, our failure to specifically resolve them can result in a prolonged pattern of repetitious worry which can linger for a lifetime and end up reinforcing itself as the years pass.

CHAPTER EIGHT

SELF-DEPENDENCE.

When we focus our attention upon ourselves and our own natural abilities to cope with the challenges and responsibilities of life, we begin to prepare the groundwork for worry.

Worry is often the direct result of failing to GET WISDOM!

When we assume that we possess the capabilities to solve our problems or manage the challenges and decisions of life, we quickly fall prey to mounting feelings of worry.

When we try to shoulder the burdens of responsibility for our life, we are left to our limited resources and the inevitable consequences of frustration and worry set in.

Worry is often the result of self-dependence and self-sufficiency.

This is a common pitfall which many fall into.

Leaning upon our own understanding is hopelessly inadequate.

When we fail to "GET WISDOM!" our burdens grow heavier, and our worries gradually intensify.

CHAPTER NINE

TOO MUCH THINKING.

This is being under mental bondage.

This is often the indirect source of our worry.

The great instigator behind much of our anxiety is what we think since thinking agitates and encourages us to worry.

What we think controls the kind of life we live and lead.

When our thinking is focused upon our problems, ourselves and our natural understanding, our confidence and courage diminishes.

Our thinking often paint grim picture of foreboding possibilities and embellishes our worries with additional suggestions, insights, considerations, and fears in order to further fan the flames of insecurity and worry.

Those whose character and temperament are prone to worry are especially susceptible to attacks due to their thoughts.

CHAPTER TEN

FACTS ABOUT WORRY.

Most of our worries are based upon groundless, imaginary, unsubstantiated fear.

The overwhelming majority of our worries are based on "what will it be?" rather than reality of "what it is!".

Worry accomplishes nothing beneficial.

It is not constructive but destructive.

It is not help but a hindrance.

It is not part of the solution but part of the problem.

One of the greatest arguments justifying worry is the deceitful lie that worry can help us solve our problems.

Worry solves nothing! It only complicates and intensifies our dilemmas.

"And which of you by worrying can add one cubit to his stature?" Jesus Christ of Nazareth.

Worry breeds worry!

The more we dwell upon our worries, the more worries we have to dwell upon.

When we preoccupy ourselves with our worries, they become bigger than life and eventually consume us.

The more we focus upon our insecurities, fears, and anxieties, the more distorted and exaggerated they become until wisdom fades from the picture and they completely dwarf the wise solution for our problems.

CHAPTER ELEVEN

IS THERE ANY HOPE OF OVERCOMMING WORRIES?

Absolutely!

Whether we seldom worry about anything or are chronic worrywarts who spend most of our waking hours looking for something to worry about, it is not wise that we worry.

Whether our motto is "Don't sweat it" or "Come worry with me", we can take comfort in the awareness that wisdom provides the solution for the problem of worry.

Wisdom offers a number of liberating guide and guidelines for achieving a permanent victory over anxiety and maintaining a worry-free lifestyle.

We will carefully consider the steps which leads us to freedom from worry and anxiety.

CHAPTER TWELVE

STEP ONE:

It may come as a shock to some but worry is actually lack of wisdom!

Worry is a problem involving distrust and a lack of faith.

Inability to discover that worry is avoidable and unnecessary is lack of wisdom.

Worry is not needed!

Become wise.

Before one can overcome worry, he must recognise that it is unwise to worry.

Recognition of worry and its ability to make one unwise is a crucial first step in successfully waging warfare against our worry.

We must not attempt to apply superficial, cosmetic remedies to our worry until we have first dealt with the root problem, recognising worry.

Instead of ignoring or bypassing this underlying problem, we must take prompt, decisive action.

We must sincerely clear our doubt and unbelief about the presence of worry.

When we have laid this proper foundation, we can move on to the other essential steps for victory over worries.

CHAPTER THIRTEEN

STEP TWO:

Whatever you do, get this straight once and for real!

There is no way one can run away from it and achieve success in overcoming worries.

YOU NEED A SUPERNATURAL BEING THAT IS STRONGER AND BIGGER THAN YOU TO BELIEVE IN.

Simple but solid it is, that absolutely concludes it all.

What your bigger and stronger being will be is up to you but that is where you must hang all your worries to care less for them.

To be wise, GET WISDOM!

Check this out, "be anxious for nothing, but in everything by prayer and supplication with thanksgiving, let your request be made known to God" Paul the Apostle.

It is when the anxieties have been hung on the stronger and bigger being that the peace, which is the opposite of worry, can be ours.

The peace outwits all understanding and it will guard the heart and the mind, which controls our thoughts.

Prayer to the stronger and bigger being is one of the most effective antidotes against worry.

It is also one of the greatest safeguards against re-occurring worry.

It represents the appropriate alternative for anxiety and worry.

It is the channel of release, relief and resolution.

A great deal of our worry is the result of shouldering the burdens of life without turning to the bigger and stronger being we need to believe in e.g. God through prayer.

When we however decide to release our burdens through the channel, we gain instant access to the peace that we need and in its abundance.

When we omit this option, we begin to experience increasing amounts of anxiety.

CHAPTER FOURTEEN

STEP THREE:

One of the greatest contributing factor in our worry is our thought life.

Many individuals slip into habitual worry ruts because of their unrestrained thoughts.

They tends to magnify, distort, and perpetuate their worries through a failure to control their thoughts.

In order to overcome our mental anxieties, we must discipline our thinking.

If we focus our mind upon realities and truth, we will reinforce faith and security.

However, if we dwell upon our fears, yield to our insecurities, or indulge in our worries, we will blow our minds to drift into anxious meditation.

Mental discipline and restraint, working in co-operation with a mind that rivet upon those things which are true, honest, just, pure, lovely and of a good report is an important safeguard for securing the peace we need and maintaining it.

CHAPTER FIFTEEN

STEP FOUR:

We must exercise faith.

The ultimate answer to worry is faith!

Without faith, we will never achieve a decisive victory over our worries.

The victory that overcome the world is our faith.

Faith is often the missing ingredient of victory.

Faith does not have to involve feelings.

It is an act of our will in obedience to what we already believe is possible, whether we feel good or not.

The power of faith does not reside in us or in faith itself, but is the only form that induces a response from Infinite Intelligence.

The power of faith is in focusing upon the power, ability, and desire of Infinite Intelligence to meet our needs rather than upon our self-defeating doubts, insecurities, and fears.

We must stand upon this truth and absolute reality instead of our worries.

Therefore, we must confront our fears with that quality of confidence, which trusts through faith.

The truth here counteracts the faith-defeating effects of unrestrained worry.

We need to properly instill faith.

Whatsoever you become is an offspring of faith either positive or negative faith.

Positive faith creates courage and success, negative faith generates fear and failure.

"Faith is the head chemist of the mind. When faith is blended with thought, the subconscious mind instantly picks up the vibration, translates it into its spiritual equivalent, and transmits it to Infinite Intelligence, as in the case of prayer. Repetition of affirmation of orders to your subconscious mind is the only known method of voluntary development of the emotions of faith. Have faith in yourself; faith in the Infinite. Faith is the only known antidote for failure!" Napoleon Hill

Simply put, with faith, worry is cured and overcoming worry is constant.

Find every other thing you think should have been mentioned in faith.

Faith overcomes the world.

Faith is a state of mind which you may develop at will.

Perfection will come through practice.

Apply the wisdom provided in this package on how to overcome worries and there will be no trace of worries in your life again.

YOU CAN OVERCOME WORRIES PERMANENTLY!

To be wise, GET WISDOM!

For the (S)uccess (O)f (F)aithful (A)nd (T)otally (O)rganised (Y)ou (E)ternally [sofatoye] and till you are encircled by acts of WISDOM, We remain your keen friends at GET WISDOM!

To your success!

In Summary:

OVERCOMING WORRIES REQUIRES THAT YOU...

1. RECOGNISE WORRY.
2. BELIEVE IN A HIGHER POWER (INFINITE INTELLIGENCE).
3. CONTROL YOUR THOUGHTS.
4. EXERCISE FAITH.

All you need now is to experience the Overcoming Worries Process (OWP).

Get in touch with us for the details today.

GET WISDOM! @ sofatoye

Go To http://www.sofatoye.com Today!

CHAPTER SIXTEEN

PRACTICAL APPLICATION OF HOW TO OVERCOME WORRIES PERMANENTLY AND FOREVER IN THE SEVEN MOST VITAL AREAS OF YOUR LIFE STARTING FROM TODAY!

Everyone has seven most vital areas of life that affect their every aspect and shape the way that they exist. All people have different worries and anxieties that build over time and lead to stress that can manifest into depression. It is important to identify what causes this cycle and the best ways for overcoming worries. Overcoming anxiety will leave your mind free to accept new ideas and live a better level of life. In the end, this is everyone's ultimate goal. In a perfect society, all beings would be in tune with their inert soul to achieve harmony.

Permanently overcoming stress can not be accomplished until seven areas of life are identified. These include spiritual, intellectual (educational), psychological (family), social, professional (financial), recreational, and physical (health). Further specific exploration into each of these areas will give a better understanding of how to reach the peace that is needed and wanted by all.

To begin, the first of the life area's to investigate is the spiritual side. Humans are put on Earth with an inner need to truly know what the meaning of life is. People seek to answer the question why. They need to see the bigger picture, not just fractions. People try to understand the world and where their existence belongs. Beliefs are the major focus. Things like values on ethics, what is believed, and humanism is involved in this area. To achieve a better balance, a person may delve into religion and uncover what faith they want to follow. When they discover a belief in a being bigger than them, it may place into perspective that a God exists and life is a journey to a better place. On the way humans are to help each other as equals, not survival of the fittest.

The next area of life to reflect on is the intellectual side. A person's ability to reason, learn, remember, and all process of a cognitive nature are included. A person must fine tune the ability to gather information and deepen the mind with knowledge to get through life. This knowledge is the key to overcoming stress. To sooth the mind, reasoning and memory skills need to be honed in order to gain pleasure from life, not maintaining the rat race in today's society. Gaining knowledge through educational means for one's own sake, not to get rich, can ripen the mind and rid it of some worries.

The psychological area of life means searching for ways to develop emotions that give support everyday. If fear is an issue that hampers growth, it must be rid from life. Emotions are vital in overcoming fear. Discussing life with others, gives a person a different perspective to look at problems or issues. Perhaps therapy is an option to get a person on a positive mind path. Past experience can lead a person to a happier place. Learning from mistakes and moving on can increase positive emotions as well. The mind is a funny thing. Issues that are buried in the subconscious can disturb and affect everyday life. Resolving these emotional issues can bring a calming sensation to a person's overall well-being.

The fourth vital life area is the social aspect. This is the way people relate to each other in relationships between family, friends, and even strangers. Relationships are the building block for social interaction. To enter healthy relationships, a person must comprehend what is really involved and how to avoid conflict. Whether being a parent or a friend, uncovering how to assimilate will have a good impact on your mind. Everyone should know the proper way to get along with people, no matter if it is between people who have known each other for a long time, or a person starting a conversation with someone who they have never met.

The next vital area of life is the professional realm. The professional area deals with the ability to make money. Professional success is determined by the revenue one gets from the value that they give. Handling financial matters and money are the keys tied to this idea. To ease worries, a person should learn good business skills, become more organized, and raise their productivity. When this occurs, it makes it easy for someone to become less stressed since they are armed with the confidence that success brings.

The sixth vital area in life is recreation. All activities are meant to add relaxation, pleasure and refreshment to a person. Focus is placed on having fun. When a person has an outlet to distract them from worries, in time, these worries begin to disappear or do not appear quite as bad. Whether a person likes to read, watch television or movies, takes a vacation, or begins a new hobby, they can release negative energy that causes stress. When someone is doing something they like, it is almost impossible to worry. Too often, people do not take time to play. Sometimes remembering back to the days of childhood can play an important role in letting loose and de-stressing.

The final vital area of life is the physical aspect. Anything pertaining to the body and its well-being is important. The physical part refers to health issues. A person's diet and nutrition have a high impact on their mental state of mind. A person must properly feed the brain in order to gain a better mood. When people are overly stressed, they often eat the wrong things and neglect their hygiene. Exercise is scientifically proven to produce endorphins which send happy sensations through the brain. If a person is looking to rid themselves of worries, following a good diet and exercise regime may be a helpful solution.

When a person wants to overcome worries permanently, they must analyze the seven most vital areas in life. Discovering ways to change attitude and personality are the key. Stress can lead to many negative health effects. There is no time like the present to begin a better life from within. With a few small changes, the mind can be free.

Like Earth... Know Balance.

Like Wind... Fly Free.

Like Fire... Be Alive.

Like Water... Feel Peaceful.

The Power Of The Universe Is Within You!

By the end of this year, three things will be obvious. Majority will be asking what in the world is happening? A sizeable number will be watching what in the world is happening and only a very few people will be making things

happen. Where will you be?

Stay tuned for more...

ABOUT THE AUTHOR

Olakunle **Solomon** Fatoye is a publisher at GET WISDOM!

He has spent several years as a training instructor and a training co-ordinator, which taught him the importance of structured delivery of ideas.

He helps people to tackle problems in the seven most vital areas of life on a one to one and group basis from time to time.

Drawing on many years of experience in administration, customer service, user technical support, data processing and training, Olakunle Solomon Fatoye now focuses mainly on helping individuals and companies to provide clear cut solutions in the areas of his expertise.

He enjoys making friends, listening to music, reading, doing further research, and traveling.

To contact Olakunle Solomon Fatoye, please go to http://www.olakunlesolomonfatoye.com today.